REG. U.S. PAT. OFFICE

Easy Saxophone Solos Or Duets

FORWARD *Young musicians need to acquaint themselves with a great many styles to broaden their picture of our rich musical heritage. This volume has been compiled for that purpose. Themes from the classics, lighter instrumental compositions and songs have been transcribed to minimize the technical facility required to play them.*

It is interesting to note that any of the compositions in this book may be played as a solo or duet with a like instrument. Further, books number 102 through 106 of the Everybody's Favorite Series have been designed to provide solo or duet material for the flute, clarinet, saxophone, trumpet and trombone. All of these books may be used together.

The high quality stereo recording included with this book can be played on any modern phonograph, either mono or stereo. You can adjust the balance control of the stereo playback to play either the "left" or "right" channel. Soloists who want to play with another saxophone (the duet part) adjust your set to play the left channel. Or, with piano and another saxophone both left and right channels. For piano accompaniment only, play the right channel.

THE PUBLISHER

Record Contents:

Side One:

1. Beautiful Isle of Somewhere
2. To A Wild Rose
3. Daisy Bell
4. Sweet Rosie O'Grady
5. Pomp and Circumstance
6. Santa Lucia
7. Red River Valley
8. Battle Hymn
9. La Paloma

Side Two:

1. I Love You Truly
2. Vilia
3. Marche Slav
4. Who Is Sylvia?
5. Grieg Piano Concerto
6. Finlandia
7. Mexican Hat Dance

Order No. AM 40437
International Standard Book Number: 0.8256.2104.6

Exclusive Distributors:
Music Sales Corporation
225 Park Avenue South, New York, NY 10003 USA
Music Sales Limited
8/9 Frith Street, London W1V 5TZ England
Music Sales Pty. Limited
120 Rothschild Street, Rosebery, Sydney, NSW 2018, Australia

Printed in the United States of America by
Vicks Lithograph and Priting Corporation.

Contents

	Piano Acc	1st & 2nd Part	
Adios Muchachos	40	16	Carlos Sanders
After The Ball	18	8	Charles K. Harris
Ah, So Pure (from "Martha")	58	23	Friedrich Von Flotow
American Patrol	26	11	F. W. Meacham
America, The Beautiful	24	10	Samuel A. Ward
Band Played On, The	16	7	Charles E. Ward
Battle Hymn of the Republic	28	11	Julia Ward Howe
Beautiful Isle of Somewhere	4	2	John S. Fearis
Because	45	18	Guy D'Hardelot
Daisy Bell (A Bicycle Built For Two)	8	4	Harry Dacre
Eili, Eili	60	24	Hebrew Melody
El Choclo	42	17	A. G. Villoldo
Fantasie Impromptu, Op. 66 (Theme)	74	29	Frederic Chopin
Finlandia	69	27	Jean Sibelius
Fur Elise	72	28	Ludwig Van Beethoven
Glow Worm, The	78	31	Paul Lincke
Gypsy Love Song (from "The Fortune Teller") ,	55	22	Victor Herbert
Hatikvoh (the Hope)	25	10	Hebrew National Anthem
Holy City, The	54	21	Stephen Adams
I Love You Truly	50	20	Carrie Jacobs-Bond
I'll Sing Thee Songs of Araby	29	12	Frederic Clay
In Old Madrid	30	12	H. Trotere
Just A-Wearyin' For You	48	20	Carrie Jacobs-Bond
Kathleen Mavourneen	22	9	Frederick N. Crouch
Kentucky Babe	14	6	Adam Geibel
La Cumparsita	38	15	G. H. Matos Rodrigues
La Paloma	34	13	Sebastian Yradier
La Spagnola	36	14	Vincenzo Di Chiara
Marche Slave	56	22	P. I. Tschaikowsky
Mexican Hat Dance	76	30	F. A. Partichella
O Sole Mio!	32	13	E. Di Capua
O Promise Me	44	18	Reginald De Koven
Pomp and Circumstance	10	5	Edward Elgar
Red River Valley	21	9	Cowboy Song
Rosary, The	46	19	Ethelbert Nevin
Santa Lucia	20	8	Neapolitan Song
Serenade	68	26	Victor Herbert
Song of India	66	26	N. Rimsky-Korsakoff
Sweet Rosie O'Grady	9	4	Maude Nugent
Theme (from Piano Concerto, Op. 16)	64	25	Edvard Grieg
Theme (from Piano Concerto No. 2, Op. 18)	70	27	Sergei Rachmaninoff
To A Wild Rose	6	3	Edward MacDowell
Vilia (from "The Merry Widow")	52	21	Franz Lehar
Who Is Sylvia?	62	25	Franz Schubert

Beautiful Isle Of Somewhere

JOHN S. FEARIS

To A Wild Rose

EDWARD MAC DOWELL, Op. 51

29
f rit.
mp a tempo
f rit.
mp a tempo
37
mp
p
p
p

Daisy Bell

(A Bicycle Built for Two)

HARRY DACRE

Tempo di Valse

Sweet Rosie O'Grady

MAUDE NUGENT

Pomp And Circumstance

EDWARD ELGAR

45 Grandioso

Mighty Lak' A Rose

ETHELBERT NEVIN

14 a little faster
a little faster
18 a tempo
rit.
rit.
a tempo
22
rit.
rit.

Kentucky Babe

ADAM GEIBEL

cresc. rit. f
21
a tempo
mf
a tempo
mf
29
rall. p
rall. p

The Band Played On

21
29
1.
2.

After The Ball

CHARLES K. HARRIS

Santa Lucia

Neapolitan Song

Red River Valley

Kathleen Mavourneen

FREDERICK N. CROUCH

America, The Beautiful

SAMUEL A. WARD

Hatikvoh

(The Hope)

Hebrew National Anthem

Moderato

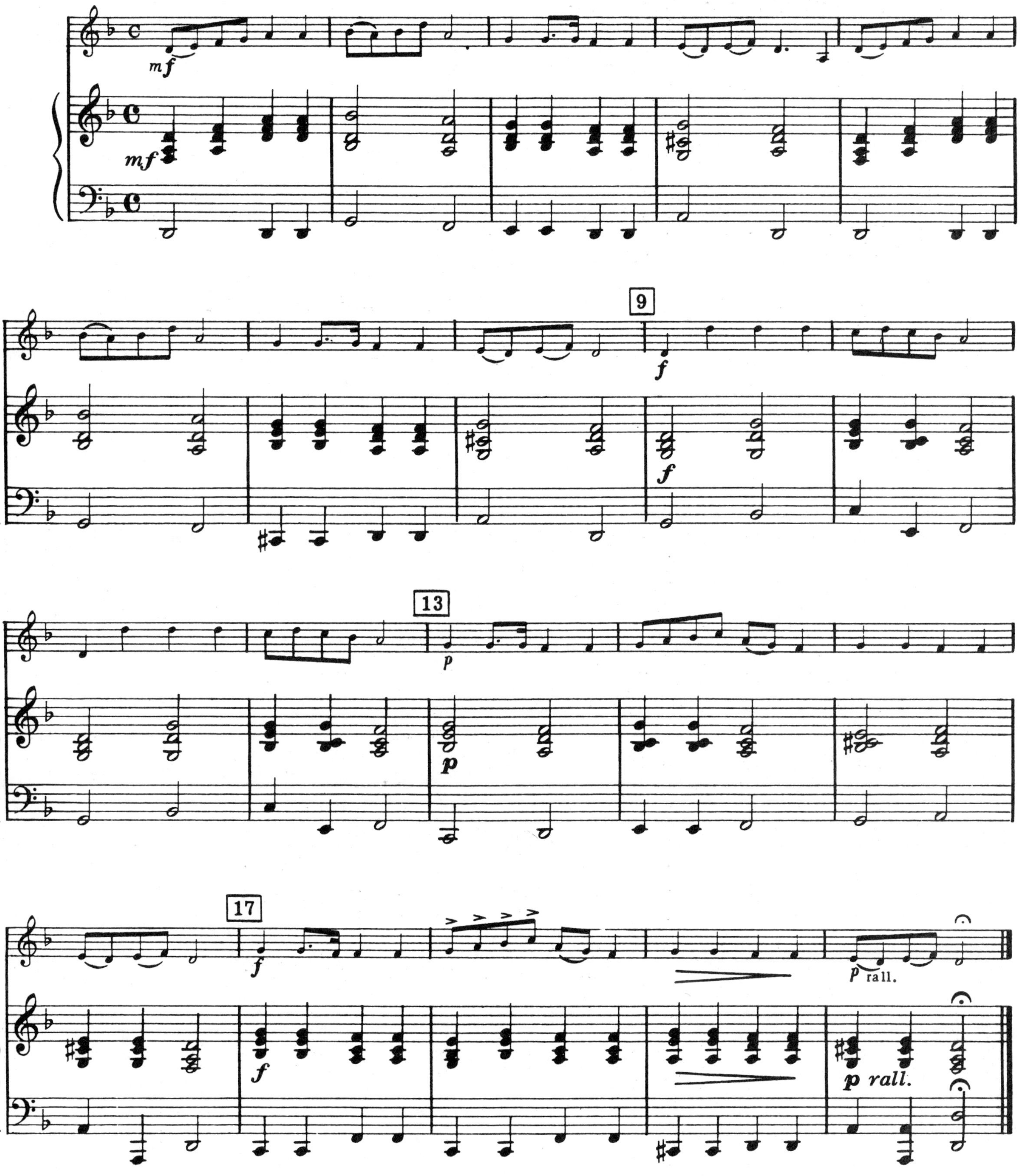

American Patrol

F. W. MEACHAM

Tempo di Marcia

21
mf
mf
29
f
f

Battle Hymn Of The Republic

JULIA WARD HOWE

I'll Sing Thee Songs Of Araby

FREDERIC CLAY

In Old Madrid

18
p
p
f
f
28
rall.
p a tempo
rall.
p a tempo
f
f
rall.
rall.

O Sole Mio!

E. DI CAPUA

La Paloma

SEBASTIAN YRADIER

p
p
30
38
f
f

La Spagnola

VINCENZO DI CHIARA

La Cumparsita

G. H. MATOS RODRIGUEZ

Adios Muchachos

CARLOS SANDERS

21
29
1.
2.

El Choclo

A. G. VILLOLDO

Oh Promise Me

Because

GUY D'HARDELOT

Poco adagio
mf
p
p
4
a tempo
a tempo
p
mf
mf
15
p
mf
f
f
rit.
rit.
rit.
rit.

The Rosary

Lento

ETHELBERT NEVIN

14
molto largamente
16
mp a tempo
f
molto largamente
mp a tempo
f
mf sempre cresc.
mf sempre cresc.
f
22
poco accel.
ff
24 Largo
p
poco accel.
ff
f
p

Just A-Wearyin' For You

17
p
p
mf
mf
25
p
cresc.
p
cresc.
f
f

I Love You Truly

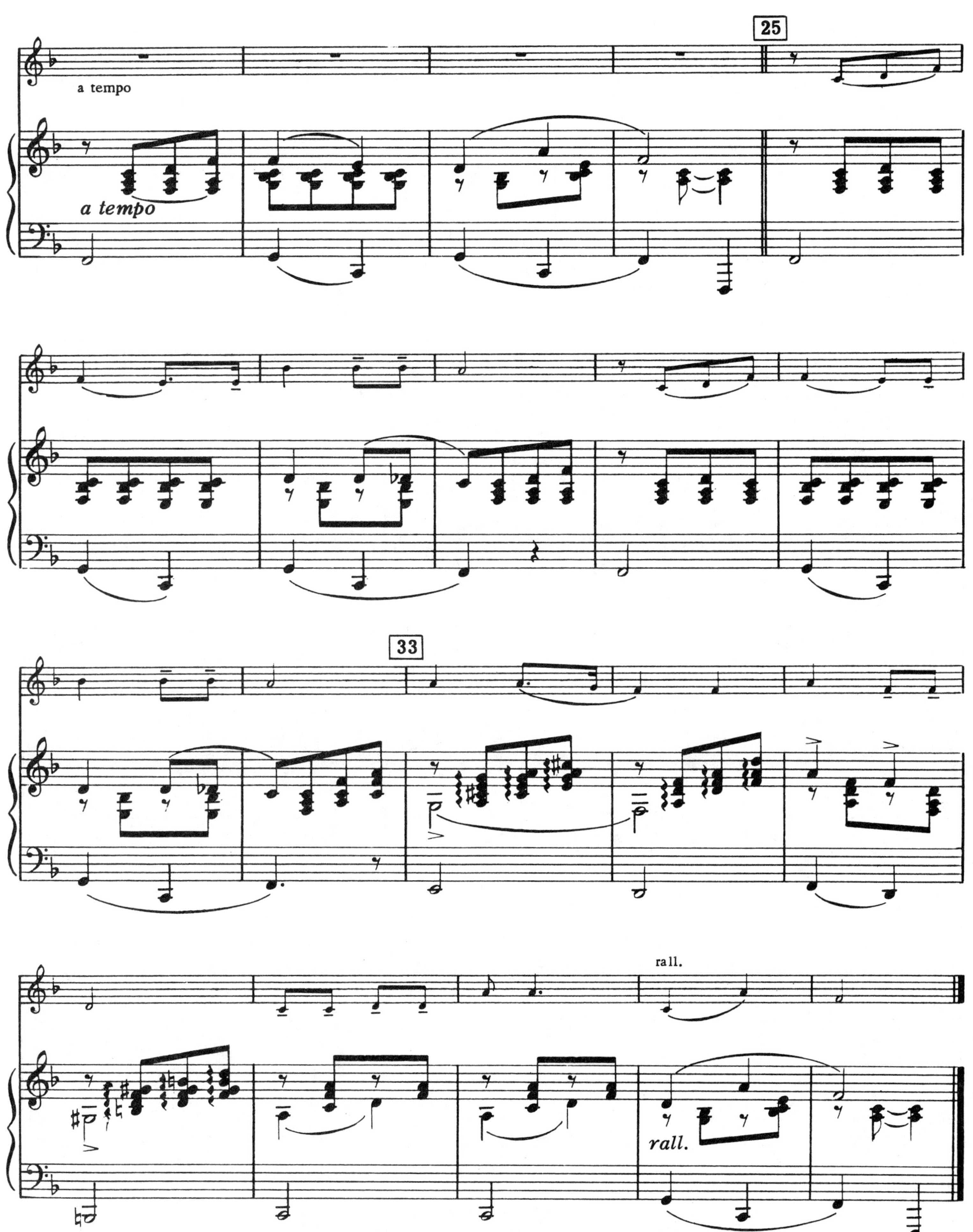
25
a tempo
a tempo
33
rall.
rall.

Vilia
(from "The Merry Widow")

FRANZ LEHAR

29
37
45
rit.
rit.

The Holy City

STEPHEN ADAMS

Gypsy Love Song

(from "The Fortune Teller")

VICTOR HERBERT

Marche Slave

P. I. TSCHAIKOWSKY, Op. 31

Ah! So Pure

(from "Martha")

39
f
rit.
mp a tempo
f
rit.
mp a tempo
47
54 Poco animato
mf
mf
62
mf cresc.
mf cresc.
f
f
f
ff

Eili, Eili

Hebrew Melody

Who Is Sylvia?

FRANZ SCHUBERT

19
f
mf
f
mf
rit.
rit.

Theme
(from Piano Concerto, Op. 16)

EDVARD GRIEG

Song Of India

N. RIMSKY-KORSAKOFF

Serenade

VICTOR HERBERT

Finlandia

JEAN SIBELIUS

Theme
(from Piano Concerto No. 2, Op. 18)

SERGEI RACHMANINOFF

27
35
r. h.
f
f

Für Elise

LUDWIG VAN BEETHOVEN

Fantasie Impromptu

(Theme)

22
30
34
p
f
dim.
rit.

Mexican Hat Dance

27
ff
ff
1.
2.
36
p
2nd time ff
p -ff
1.
2.
ff

The Glow Worm

PAUL LINCKE

Contents

Beautiful Isle Of Somewhere

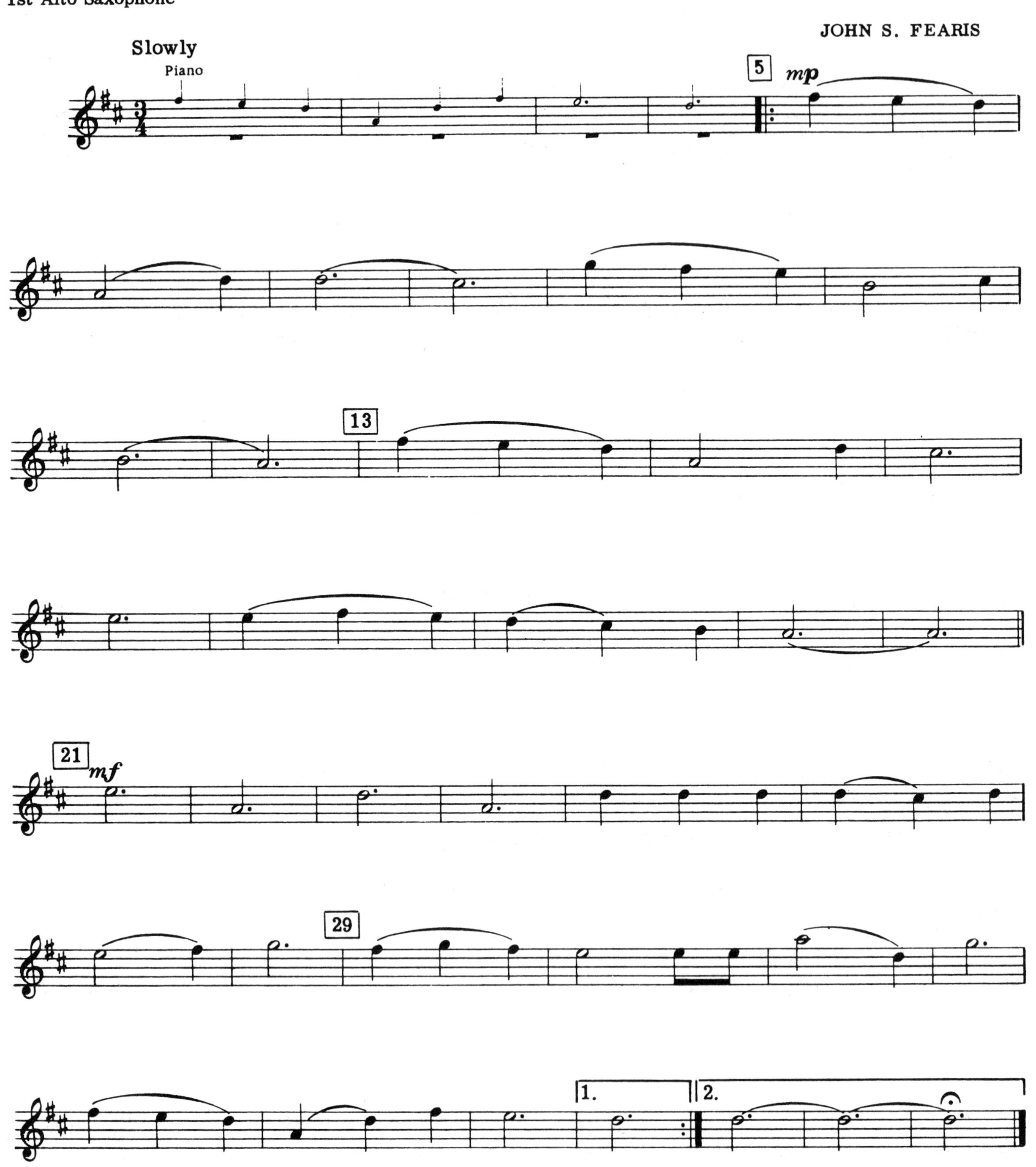

To A Wild Rose

Daisy Bell

(A Bicycle Built for Two)

1st Alto Saxophone

HARRY DACRE

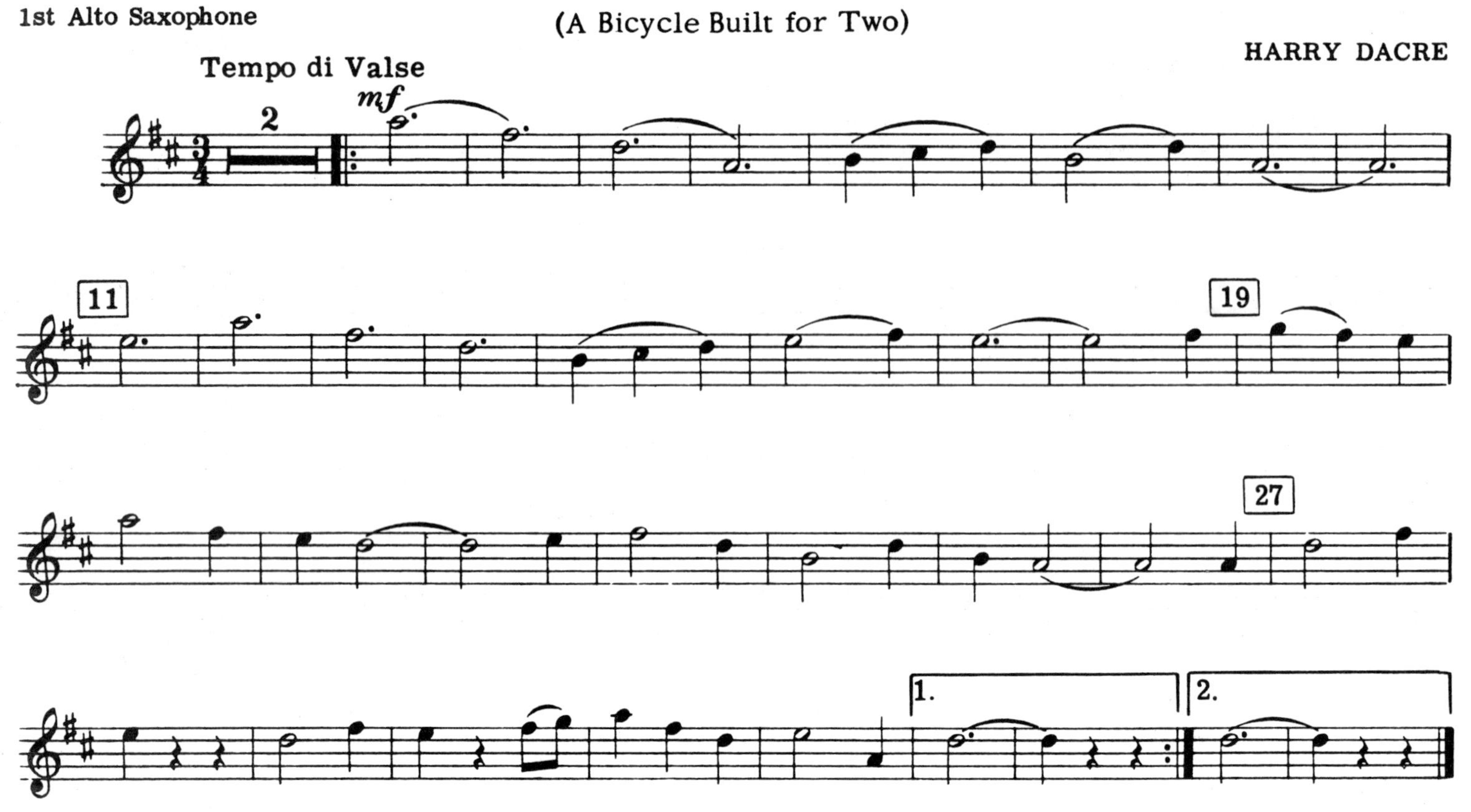

Sweet Rosie O'Grady

MAUDE NUGENT

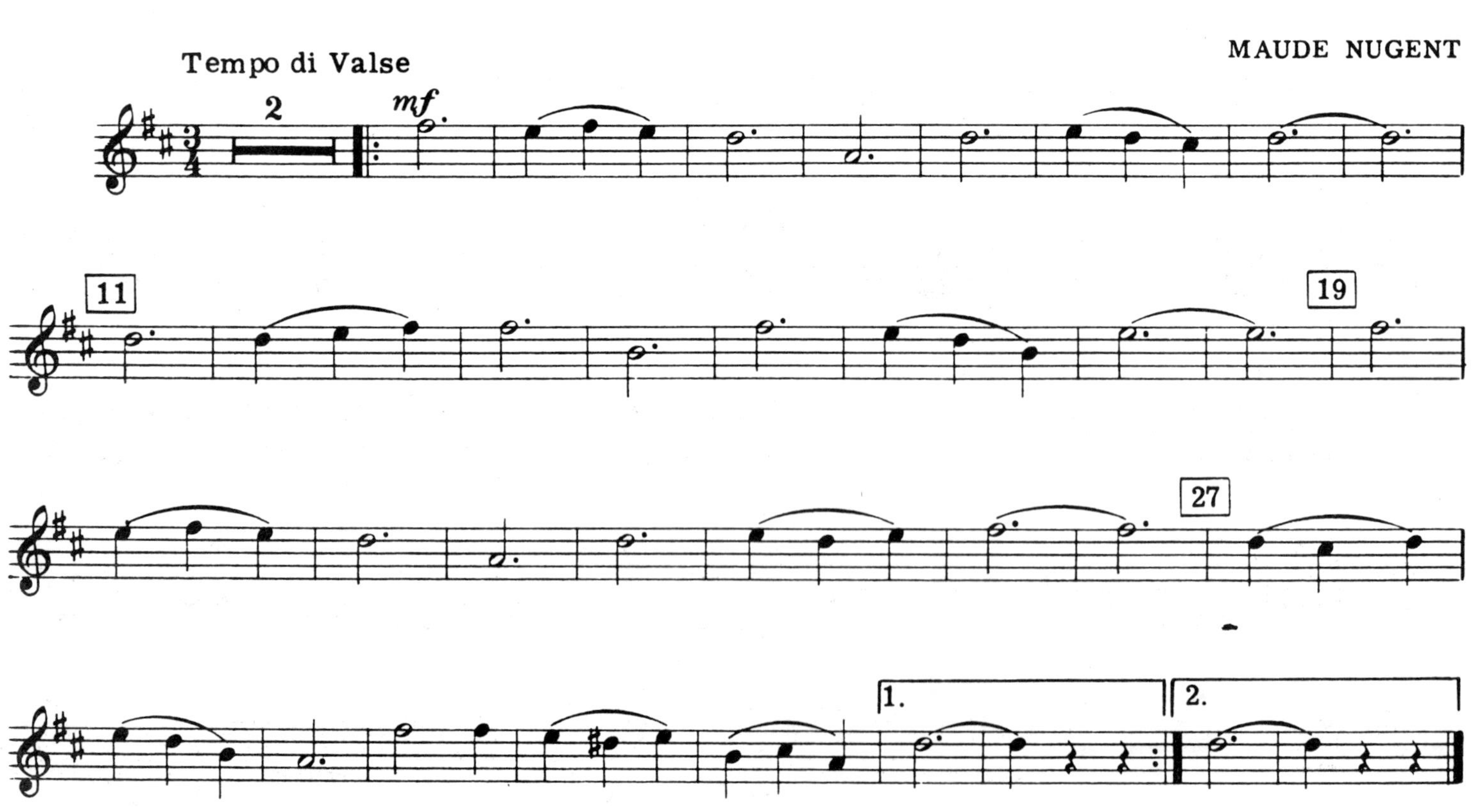

Pomp And Circumstance

1st Alto Saxophone

EDWARD ELGAR

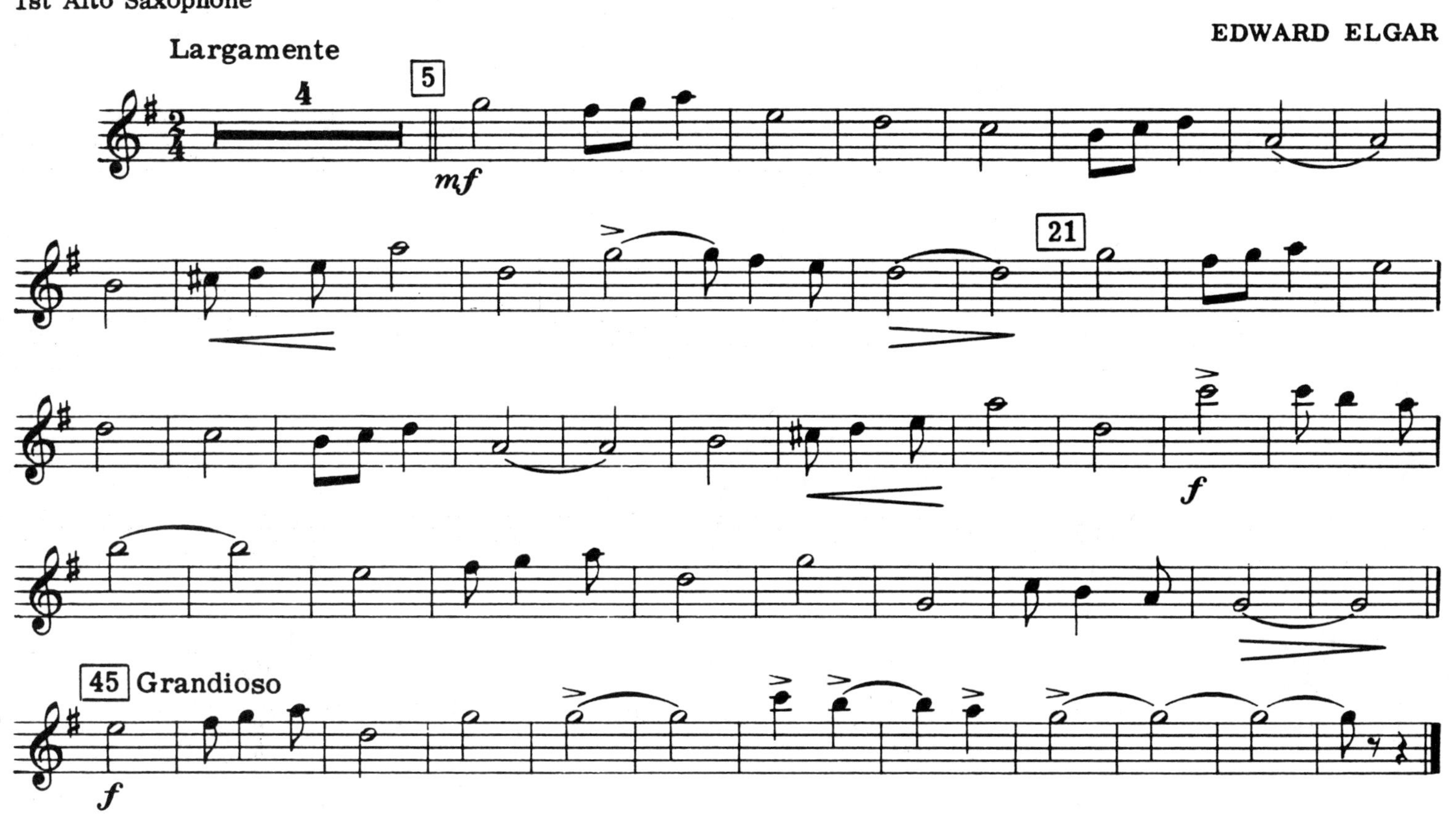

Mighty Lak' A Rose

ETHELBERT NEVIN

Kentucky Babe

1st Alto Saxophone

ADAM GEIBEL

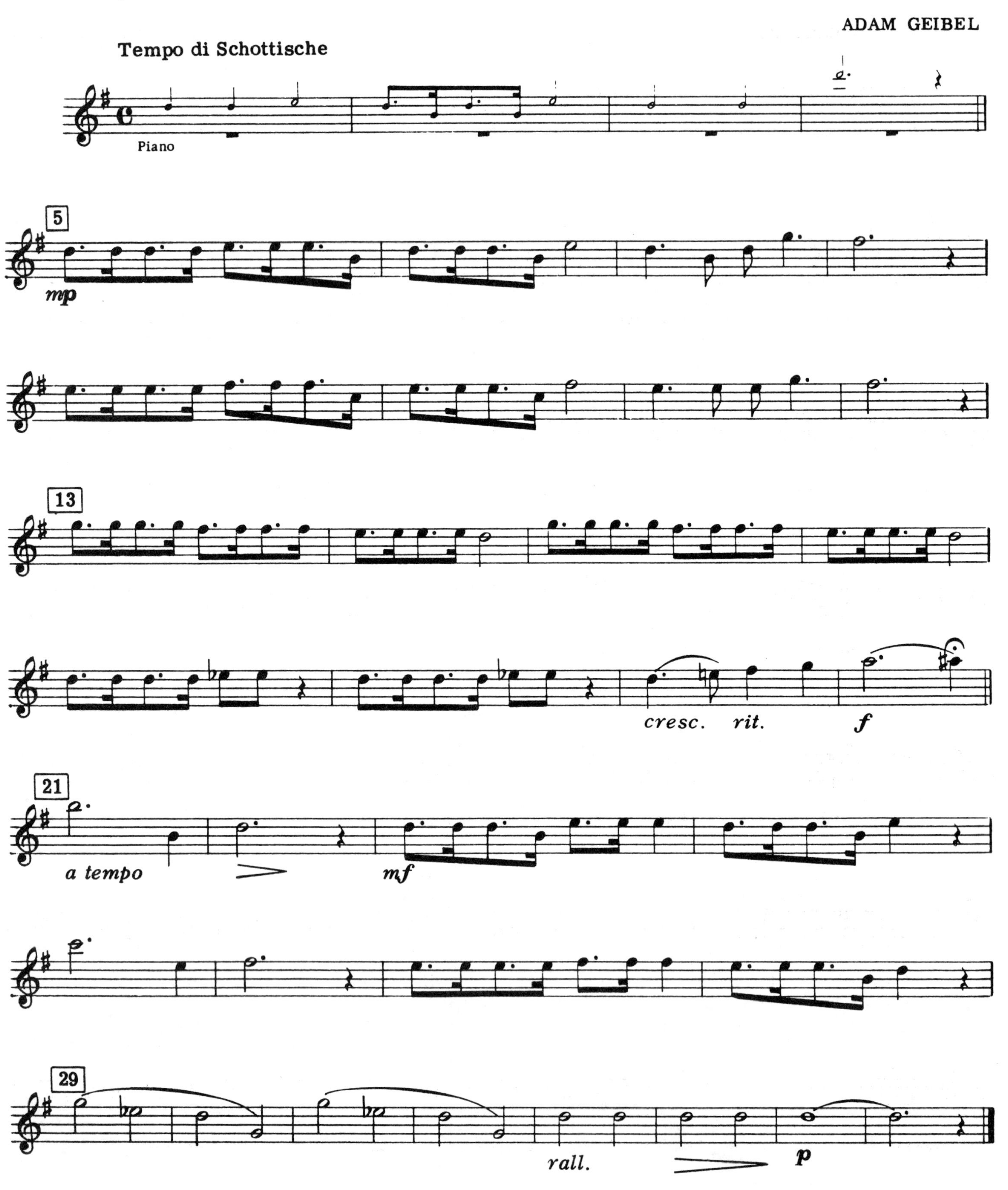

Copyright © 1960 AMSCO MUSIC PUBLISHING CO.
All Rights Reserved.   International Copyright Secured.

The Band Played On

1st Alto Saxophone

Tempo di Valse

CHARLES E. WARD

After The Ball

1st Alto Saxophone

CHARLES K. HARRIS

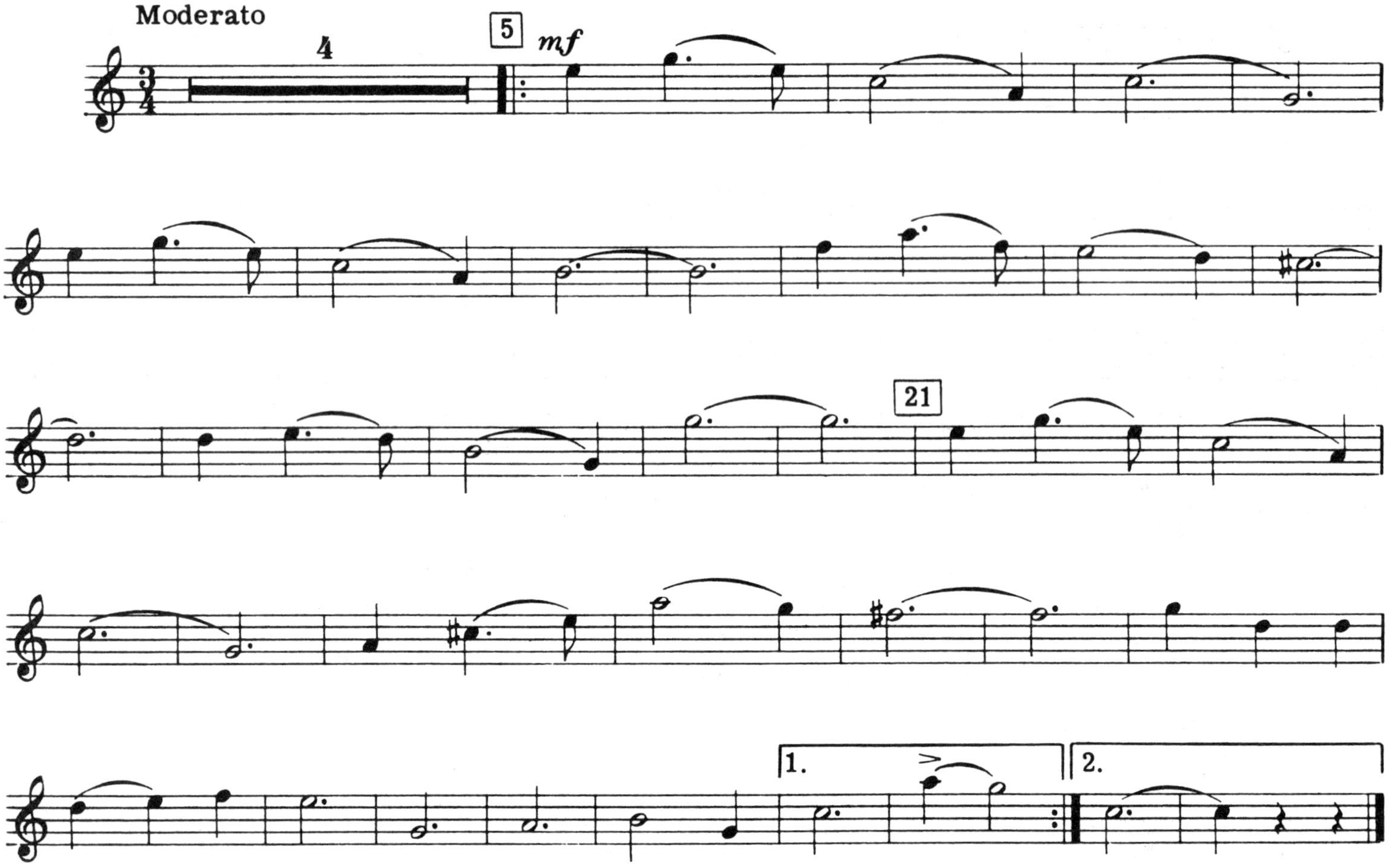

Santa Lucia

Neapolitan Song

Red River Valley

1st Alto Saxophone

Slowly

Cowboy Song

Kathleen Mavourneen

Andante

FREDERICK N. CROUCH

America, The Beautiful

1st Alto Saxophone

SAMUEL A. WARD

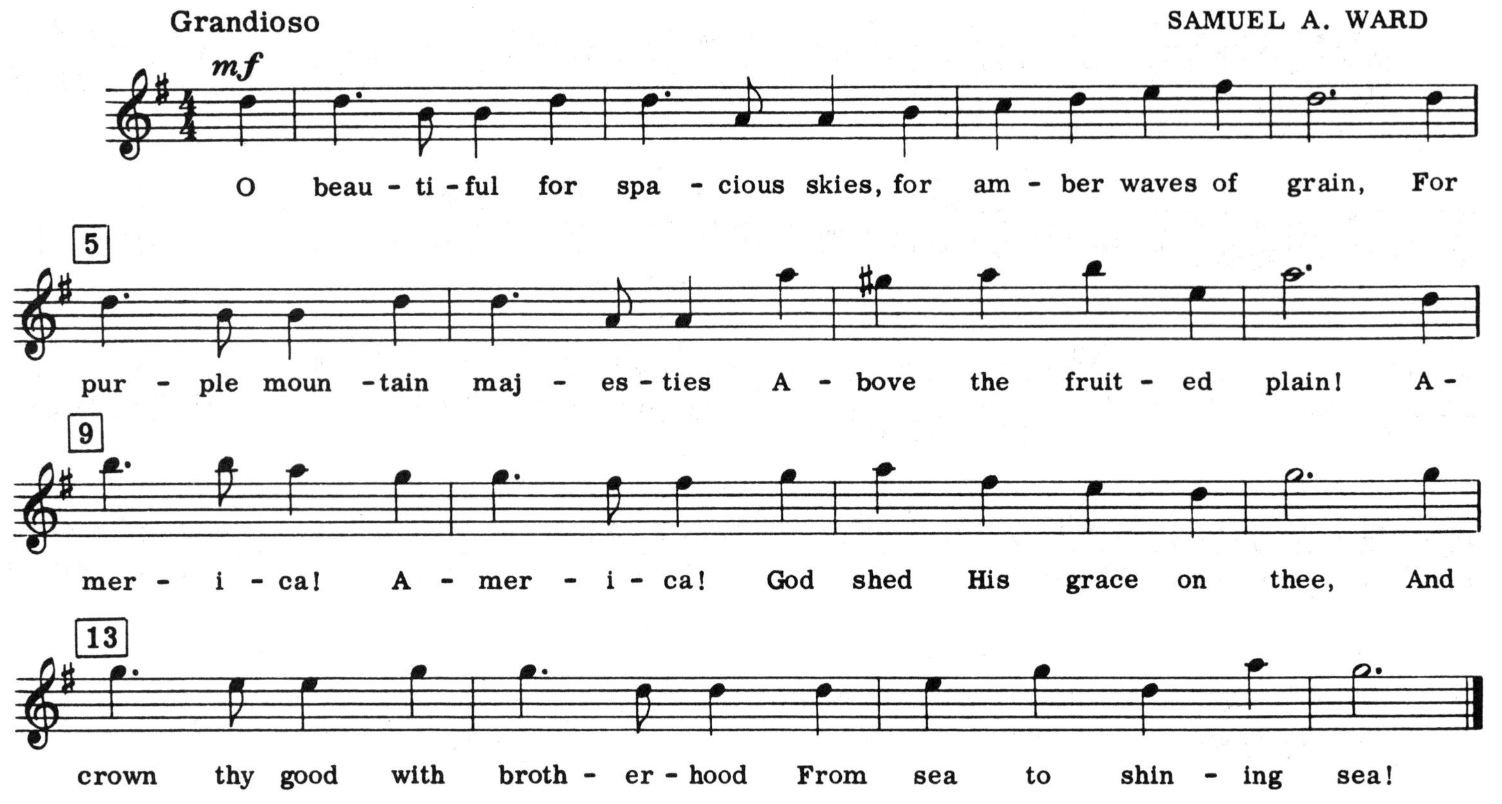

Hatikvoh
(The Hope)

Hebrew National Anthem

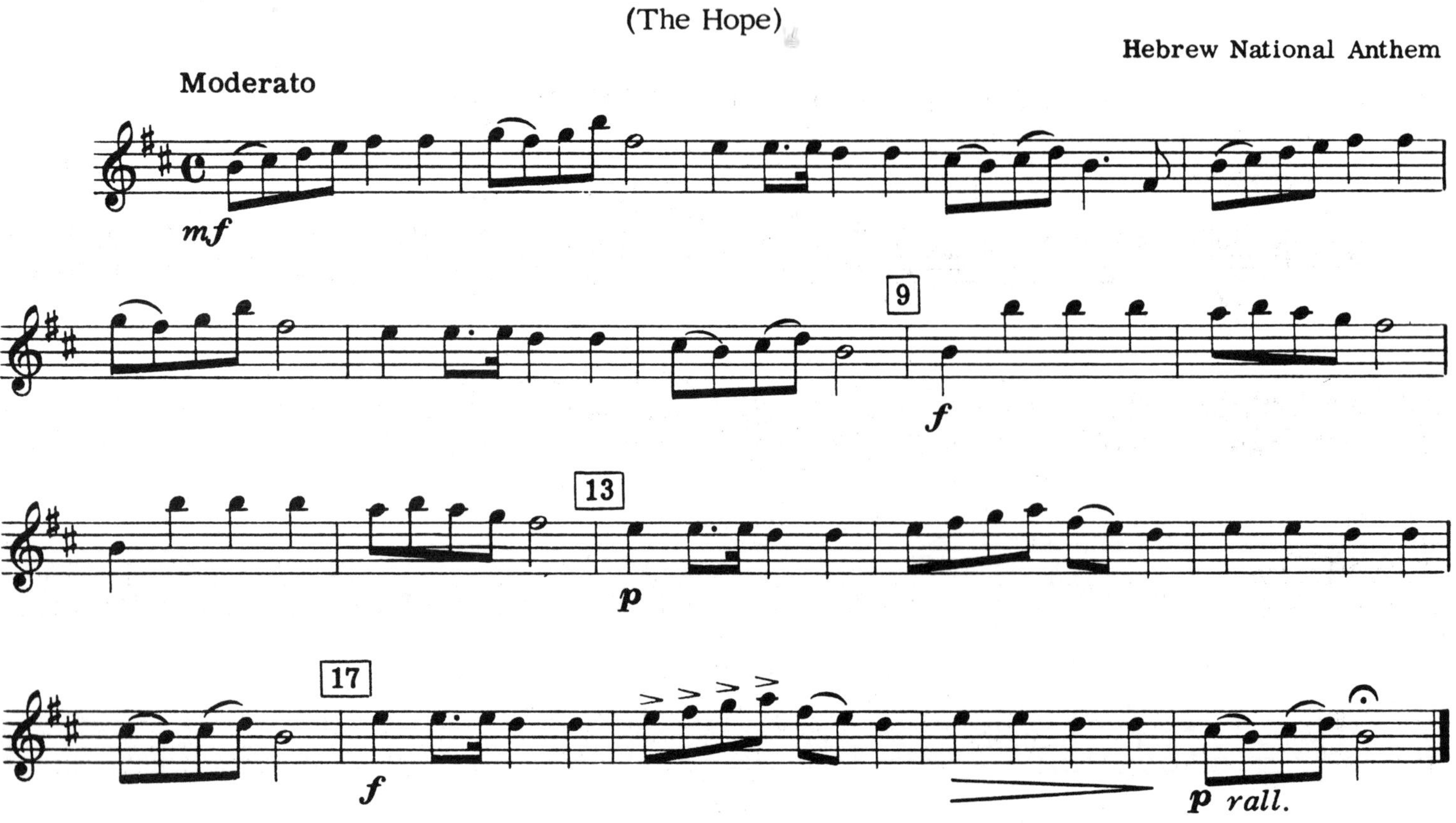

American Patrol

1st Alto Saxophone

F. W. MEACHAM

Tempo di Marcia

Battle Hymn Of The Republic

JULIA WARD HOWE

Moderato

I'll Sing Thee Songs Of Araby

1st Alto Saxophone

FREDERIC CLAY

Andantino

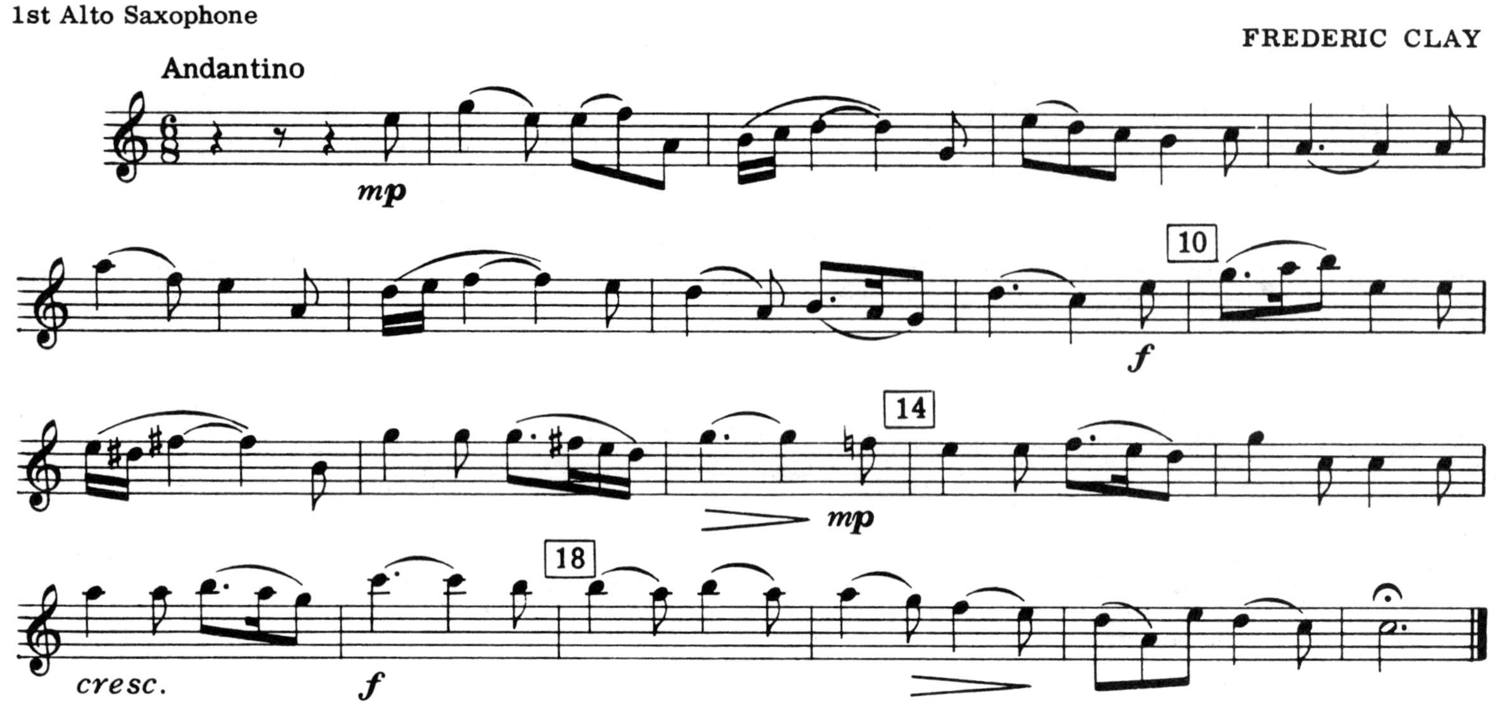

In Old Madrid

Tempo di Bolero

H. TROTERE

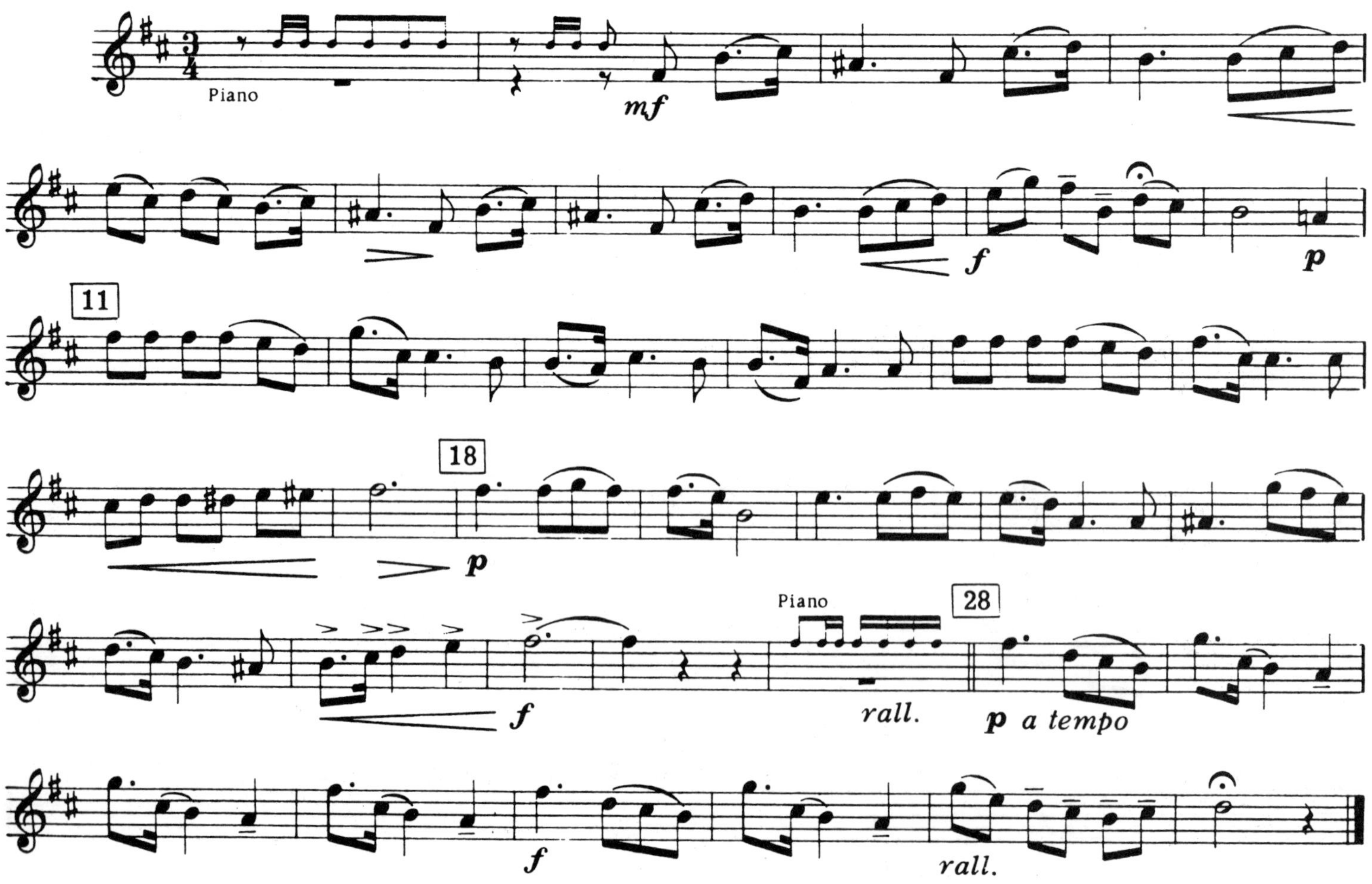

O Sole Mio!

1st Alto Saxophone

E. DI CAPUA

Andante

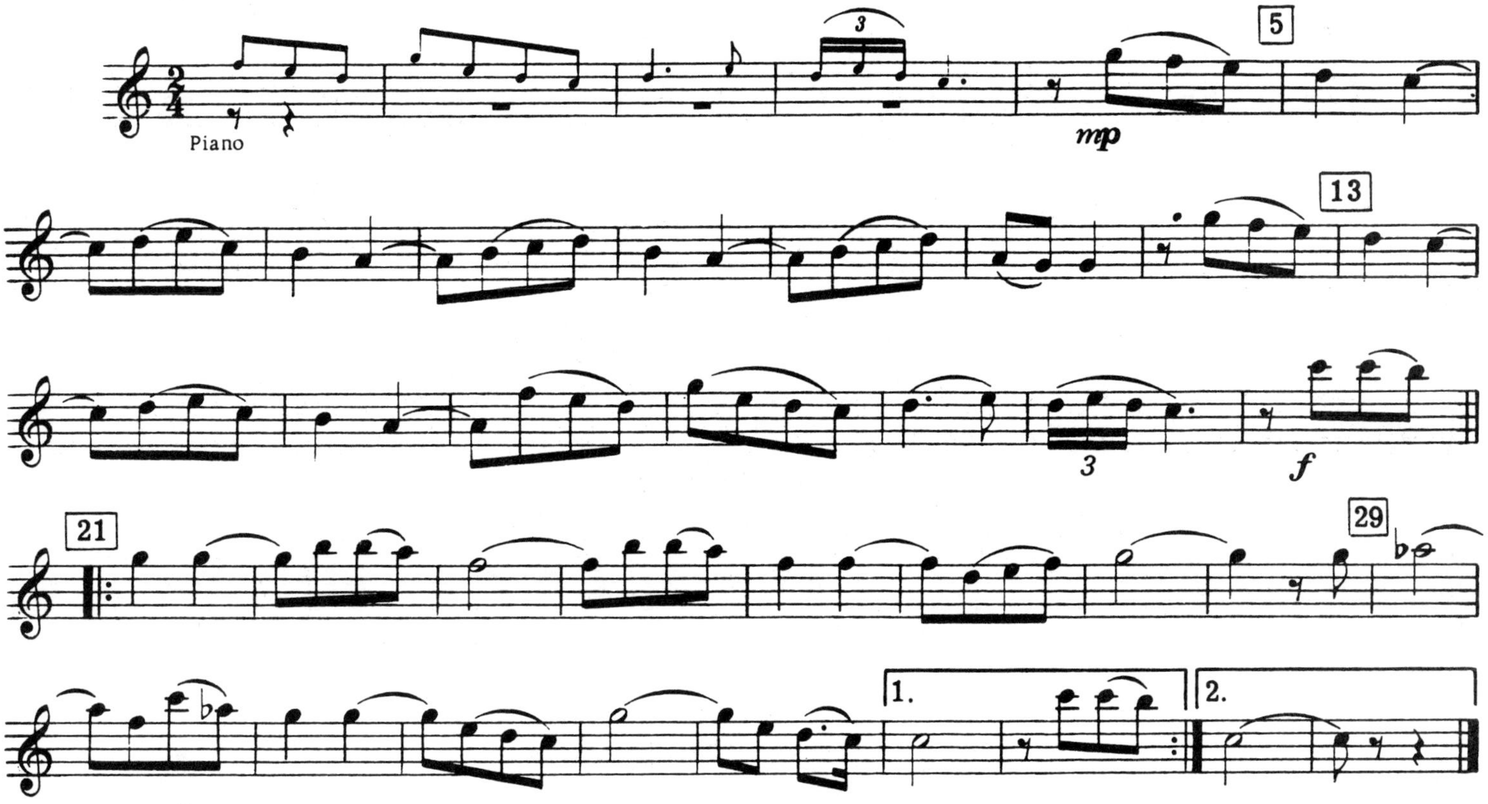

La Paloma

Andante

SEBASTIAN YRADIER

La Spagnola

1st Alto Saxophone

VINCENZO DI CHIARA

La Cumparsita

Adios Muchachos

1st Alto Saxophone

CARLOS SANDERS

Tango

El Choclo

1st Alto Saxophone

Tango

A. G. VILLOLDO

Oh Promise Me

1st Alto Saxophone

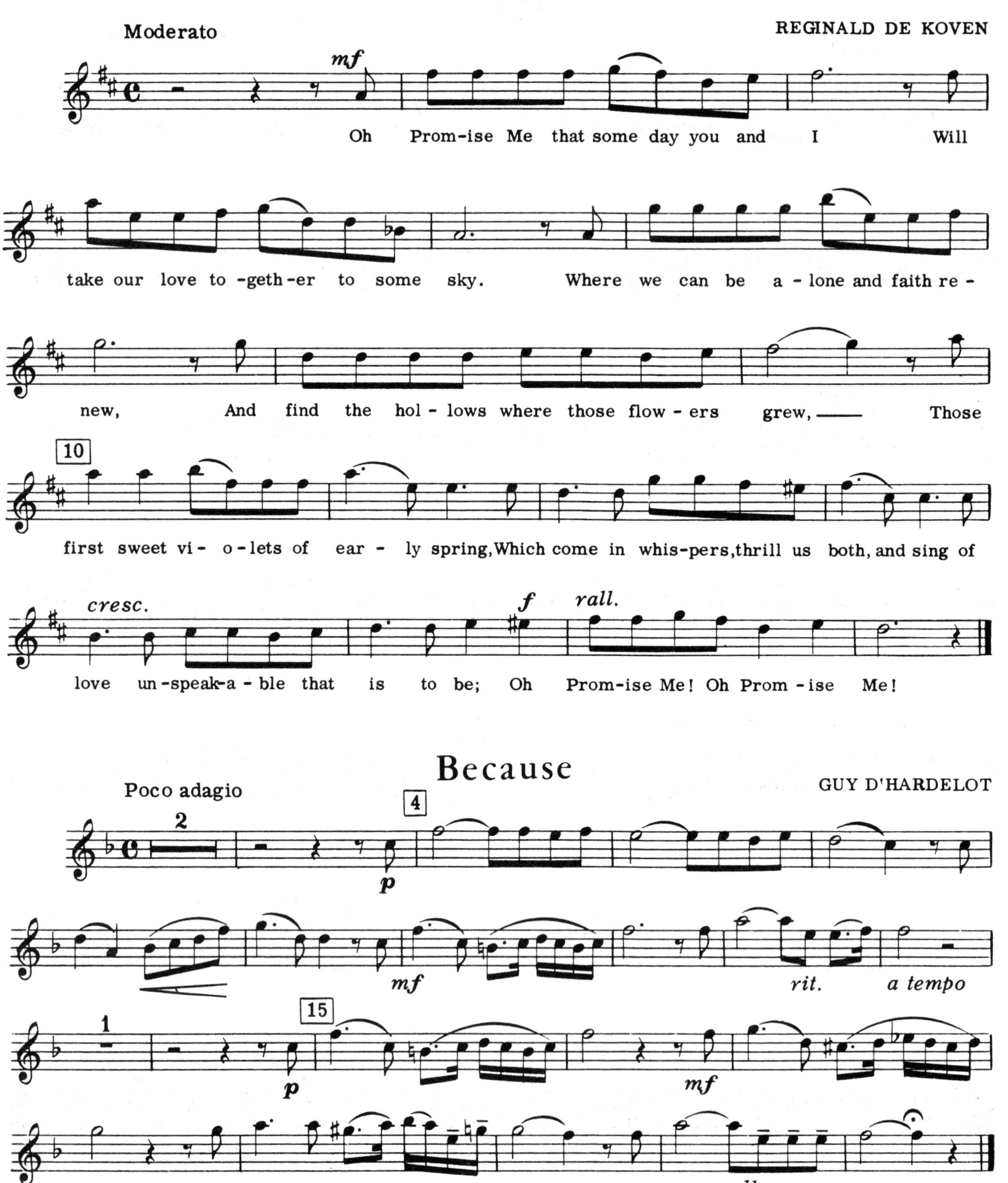

The Rosary

1st Alto Saxophone

ETHELBERT NEVIN

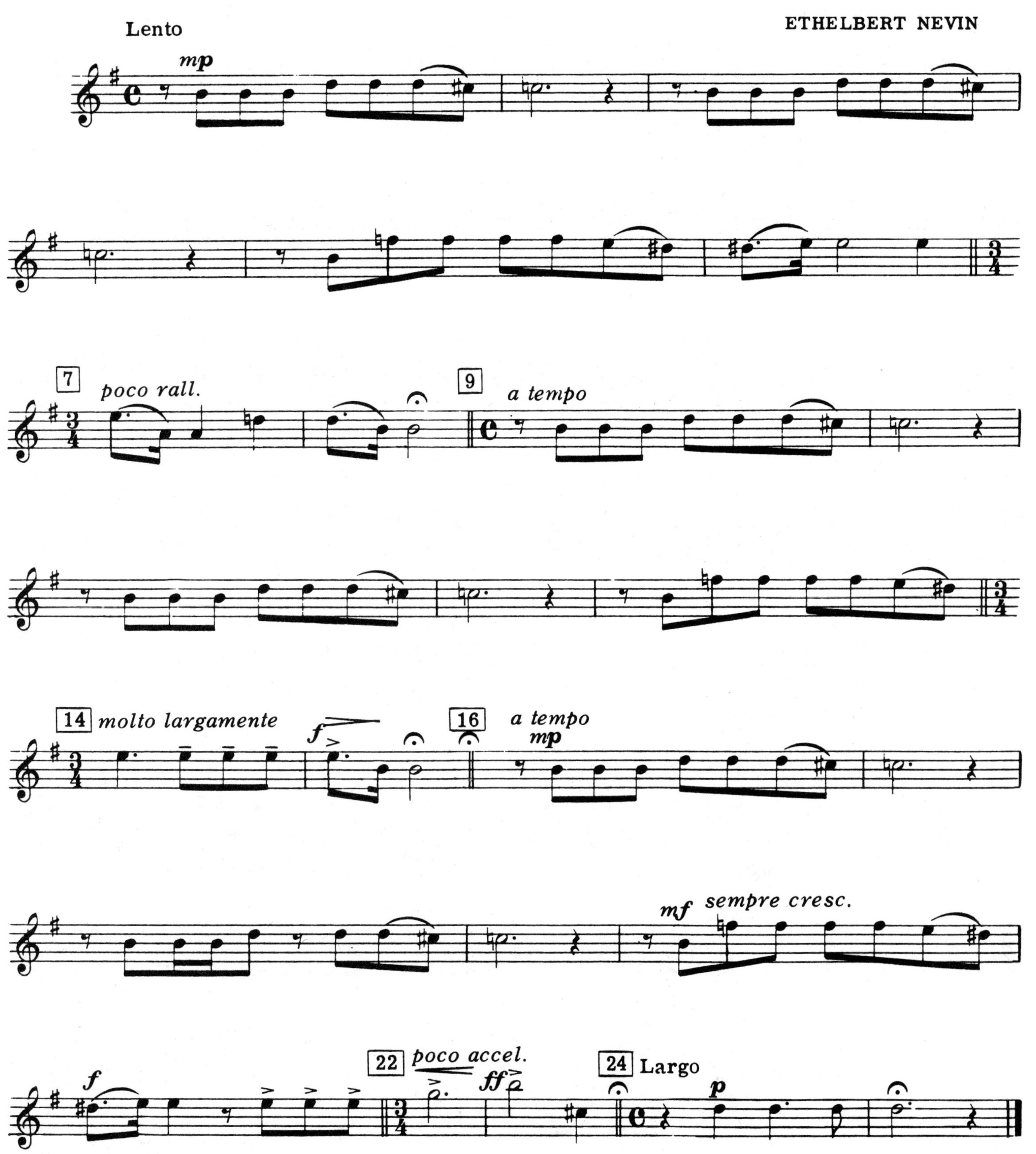

Just A-Wearyin' For You

1st Alto Saxophone

CARRIE JACOBS-BOND

I Love You Truly

CARRIE JACOBS-BOND

1st Alto Saxophone

Vilia

(from "The Merry Widow")

FRANZ LEHAR

Moderato

The Holy City

STEPHEN ADAMS

Andante moderato

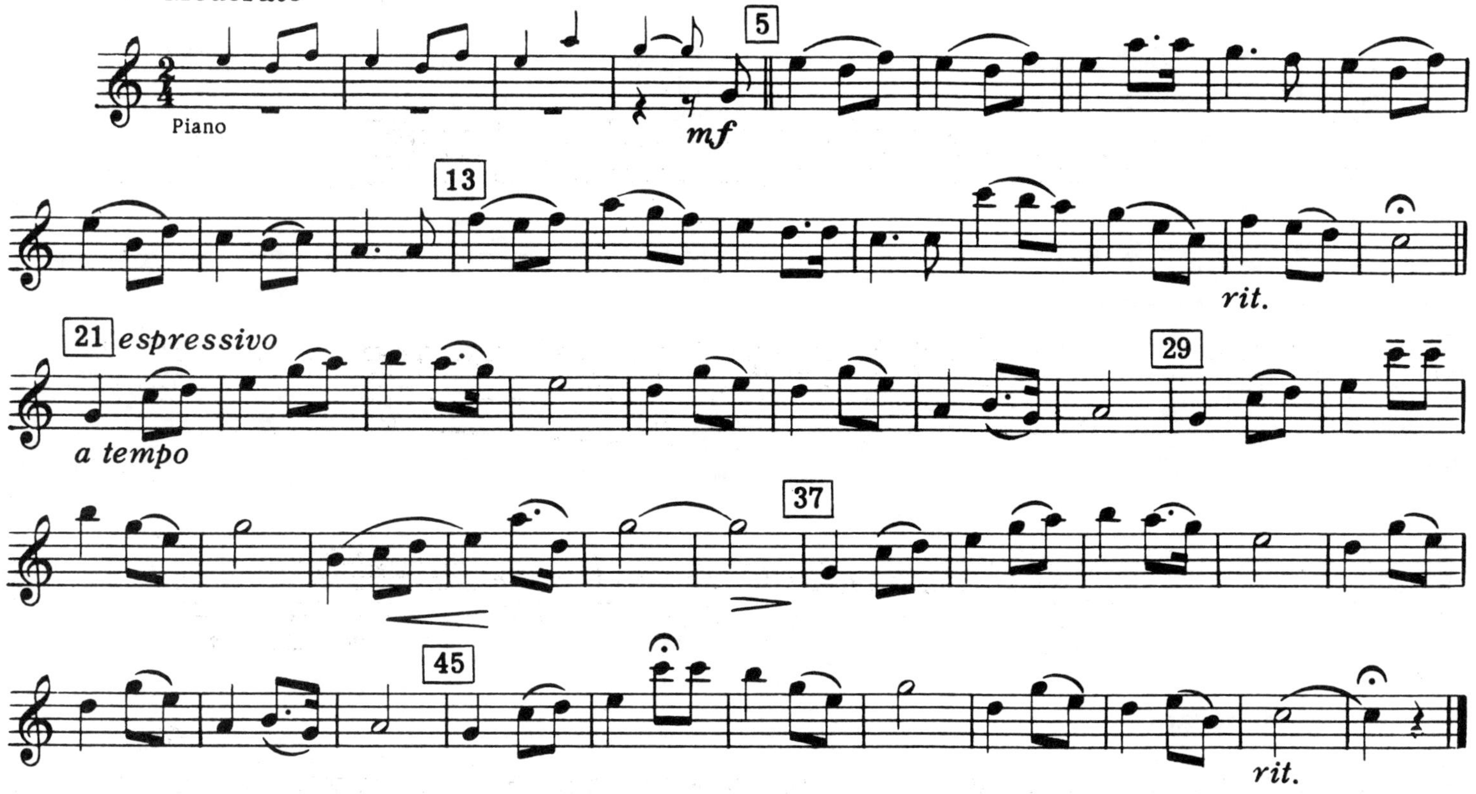

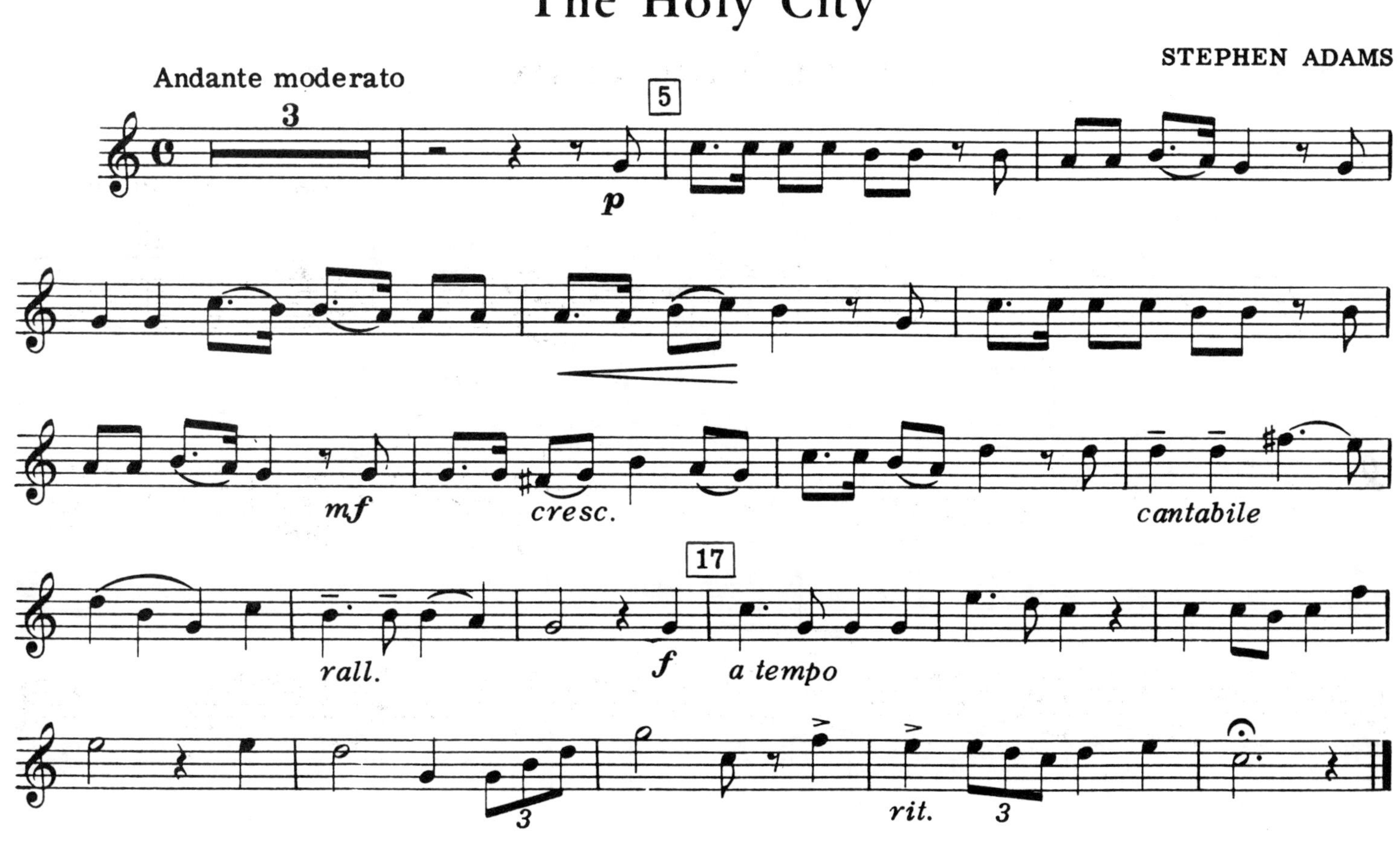

Gypsy Love Song

(from "The Fortune Teller")

1st Alto Saxophone

VICTOR HERBERT

Slowly

Marche Slave

P. I. TSCHAIKOWSKY, op. 31

Moderato

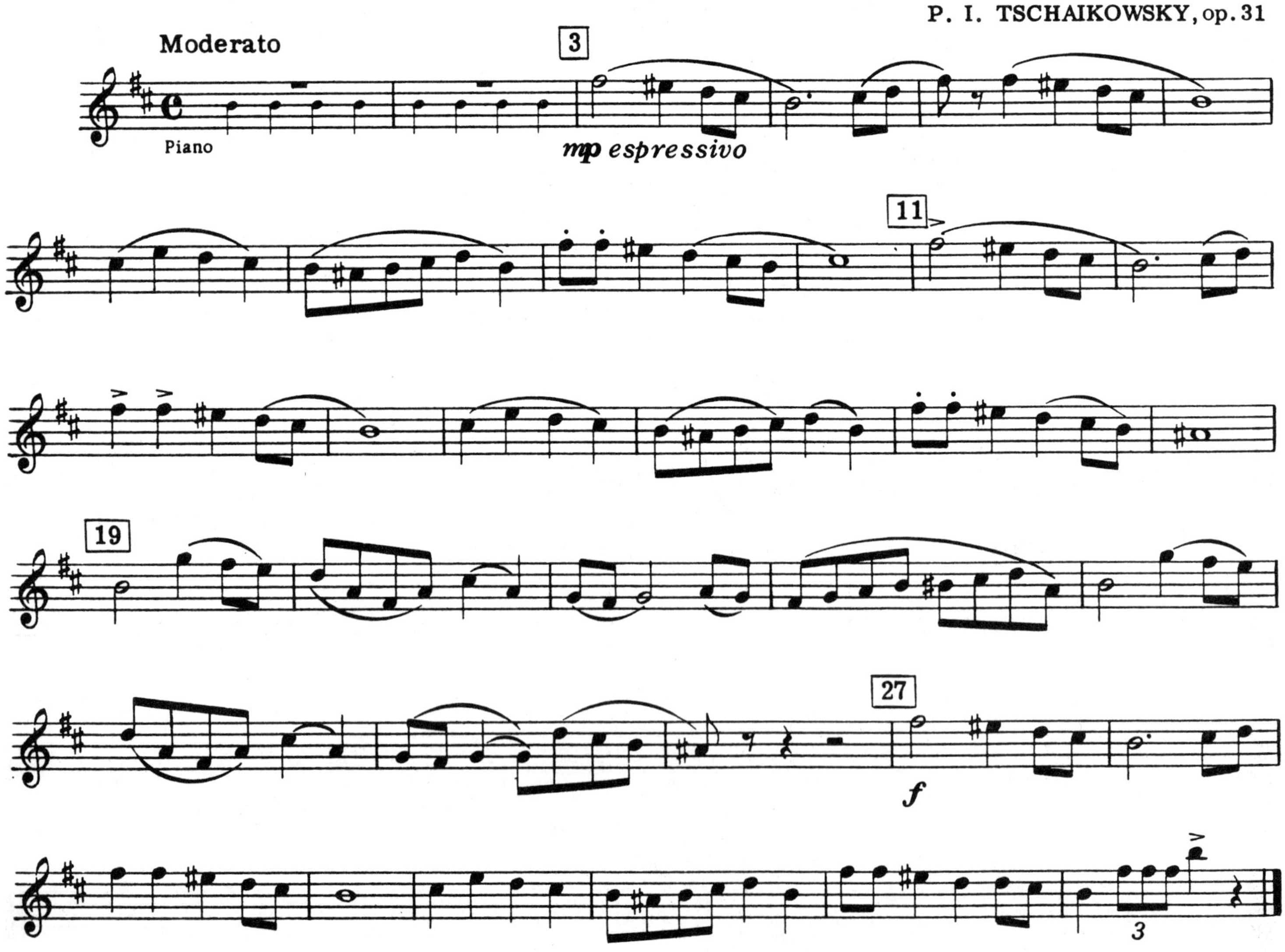

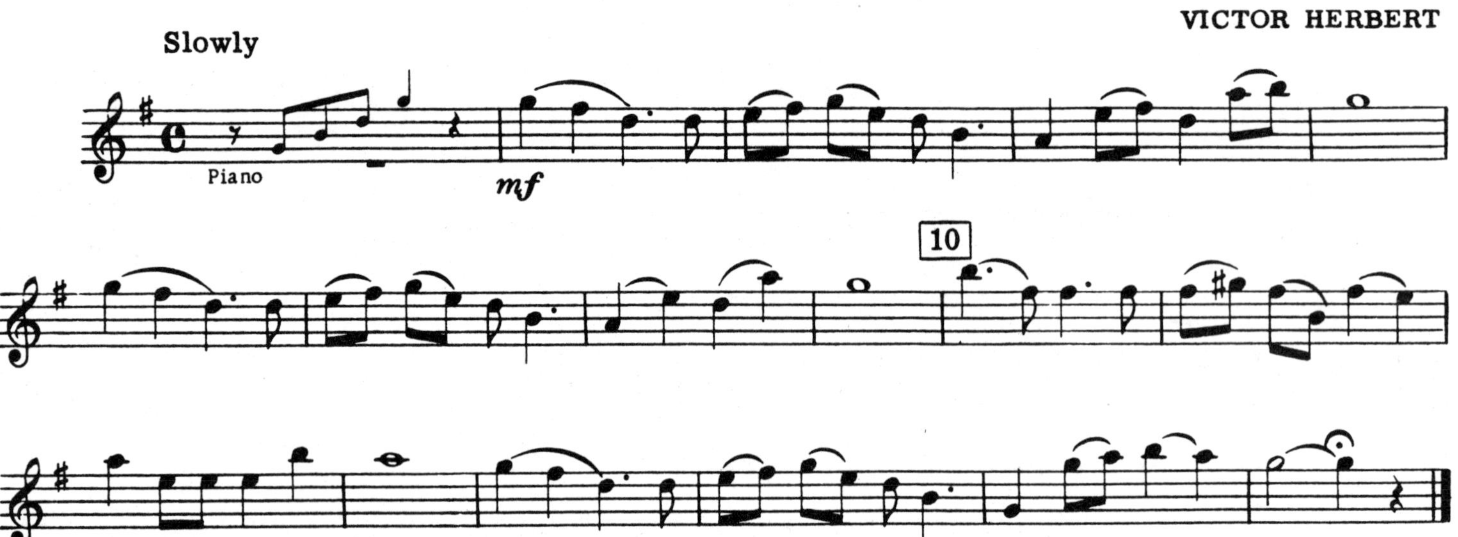

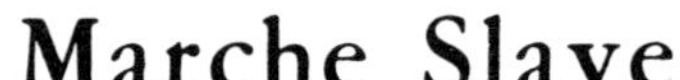

Ah! So Pure
(from "Martha")

1st Alto Saxophone

FRIEDRICH VON FLOTOW

Eili, Eili

1st Alto Saxophone
Hebrew Melody
Andante
mp
mf
f
p
ff

Who Is Sylvia?

1st Alto Saxophone

FRANZ SCHUBERT

Moderato

Theme

(from Piano Concerto, Op. 16)

EDVARD GRIEG

Moderato

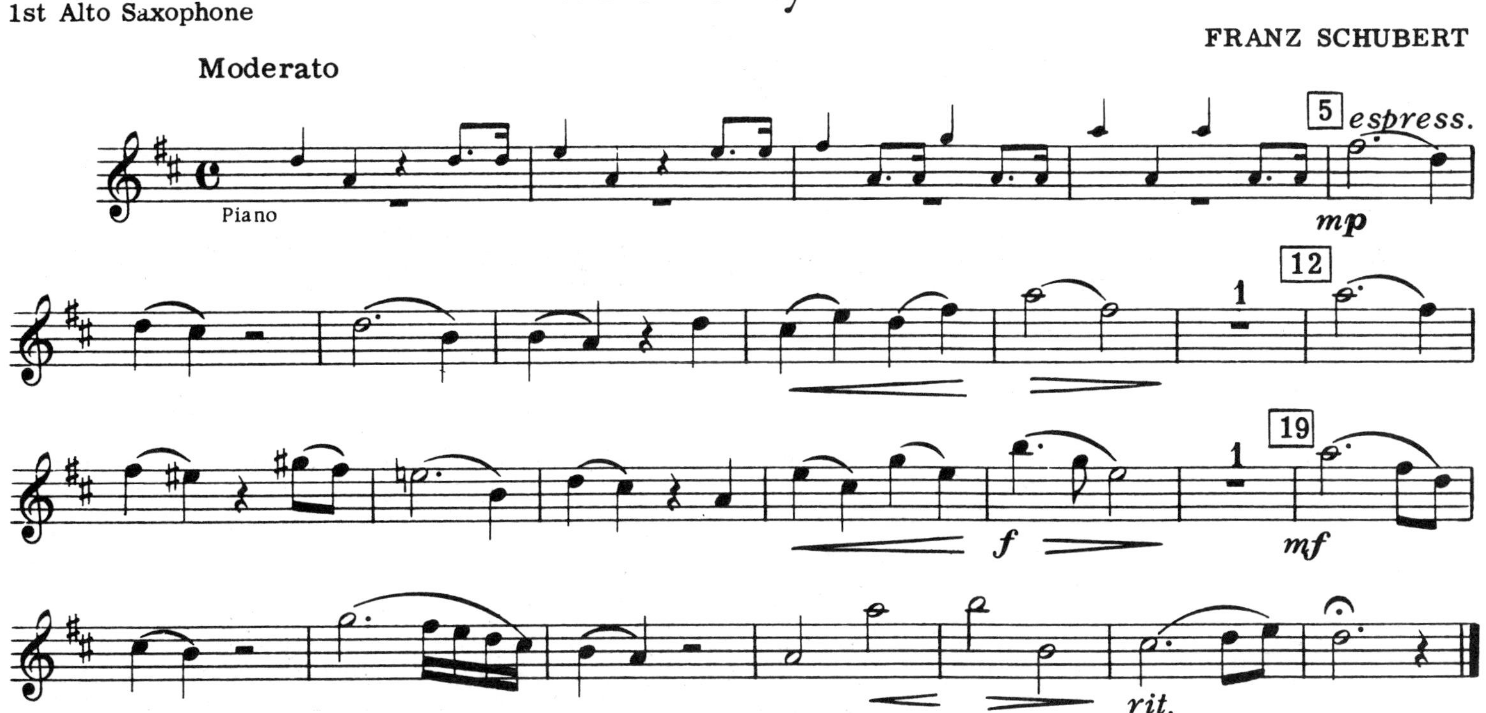

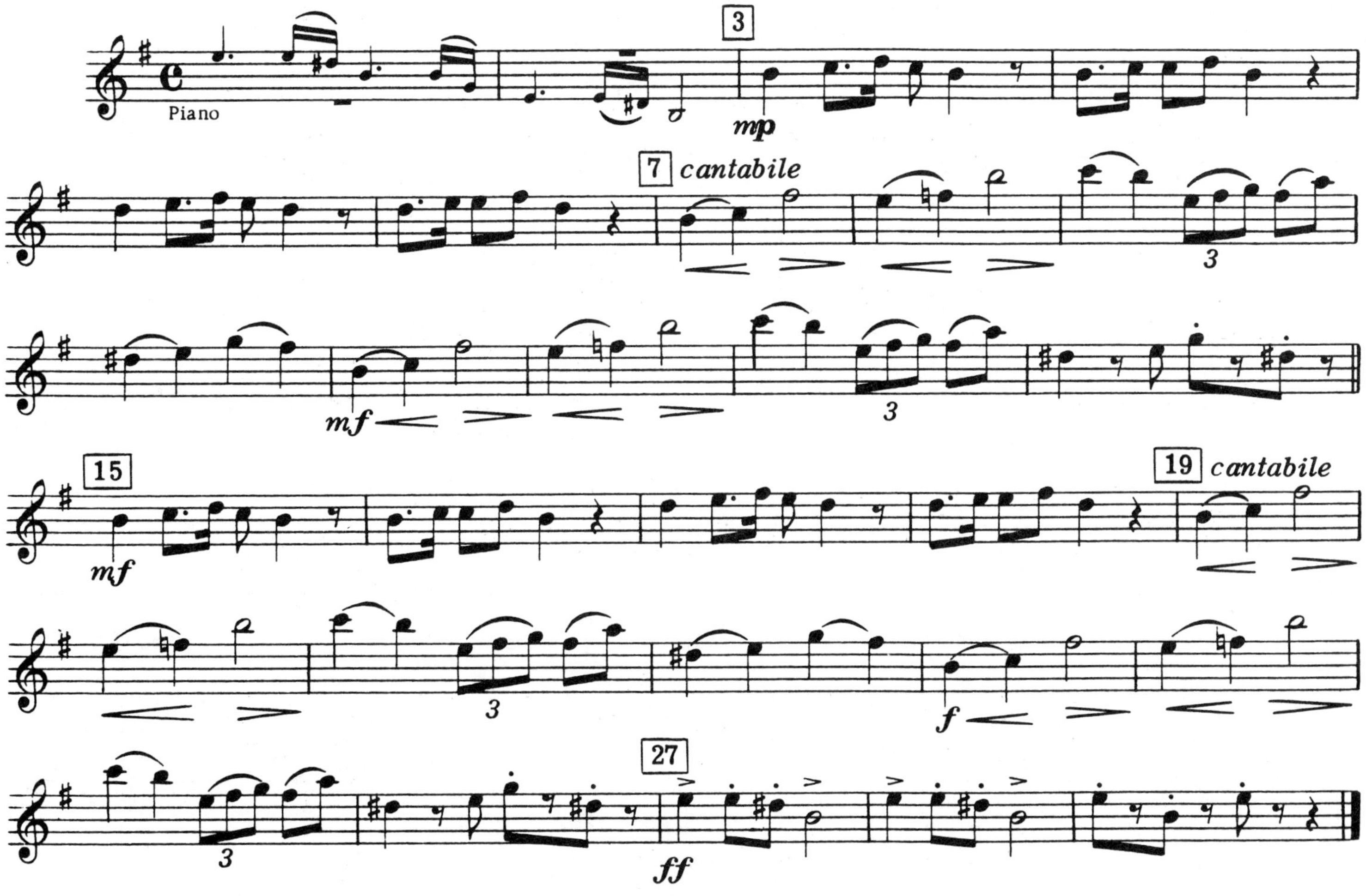

1st Alto Saxophone

Song Of India

N. RIMSKY-KORSAKOFF

Andantino

Serenade

VICTOR HERBERT

Andante grazioso

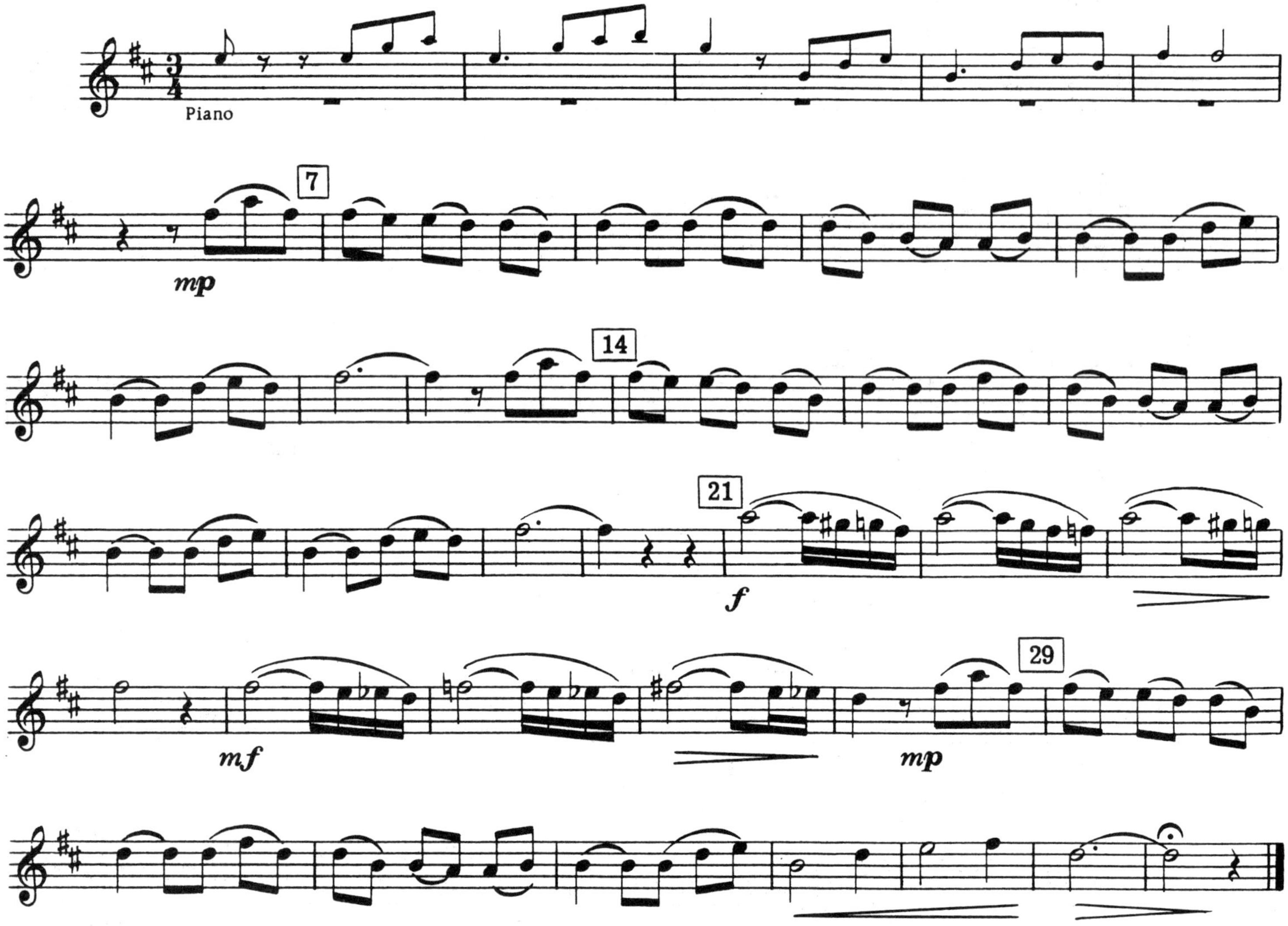

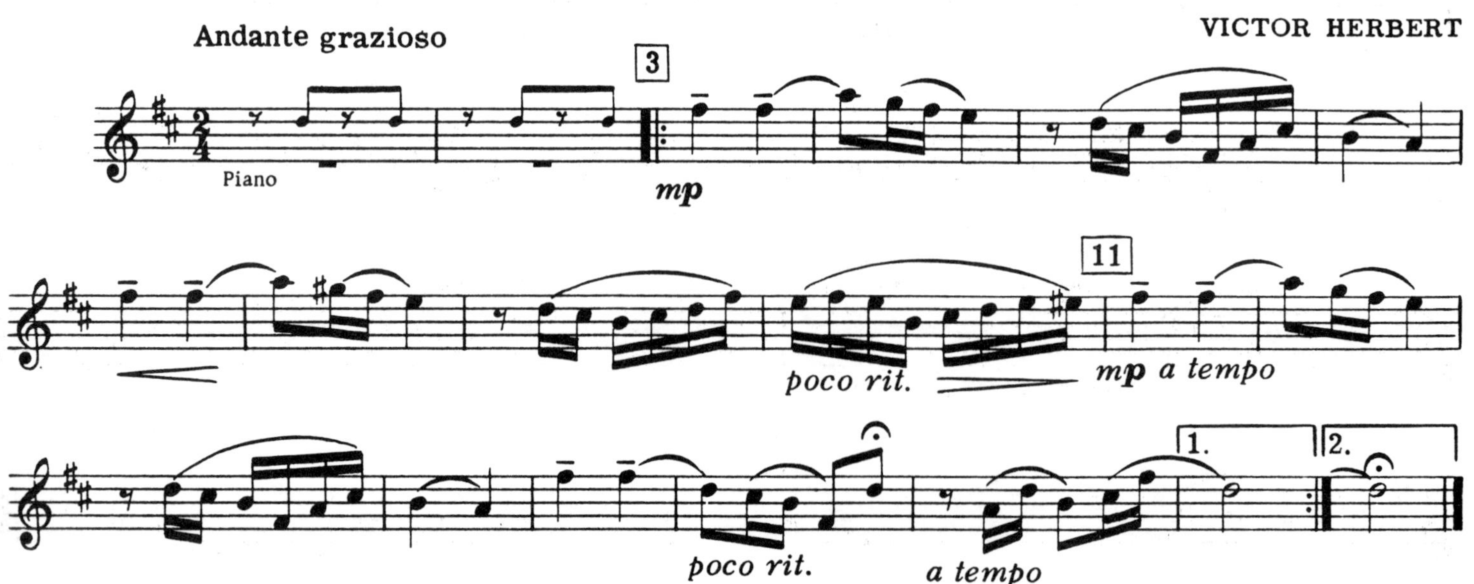

Finlandia

1st Alto Saxophone

Andante sostenuto

JEAN SIBELIUS

Theme
(from Piano Concerto, No. 2, Op. 18)

SERGEI RACHMANINOFF

Moderato

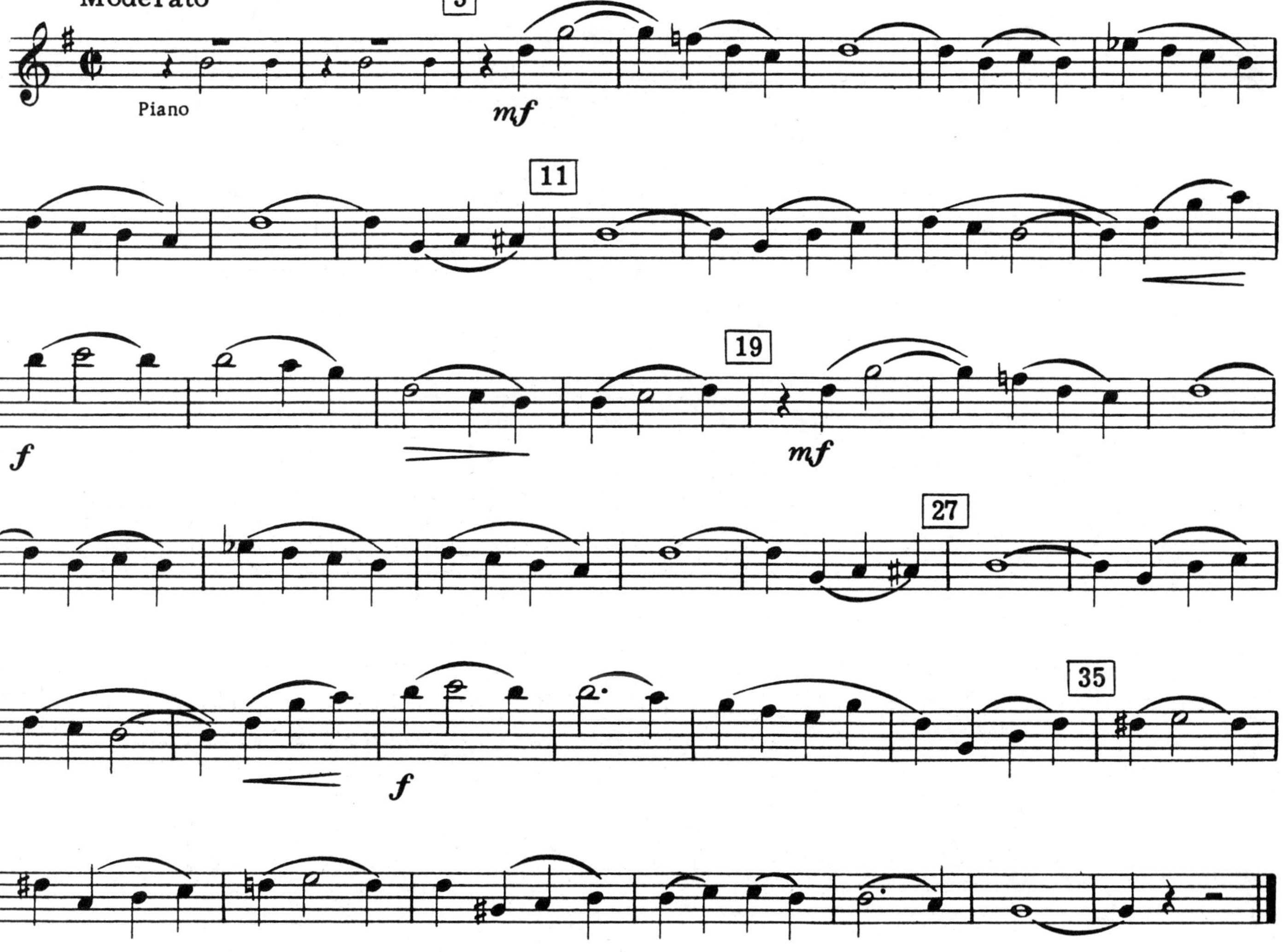

Für Elise

1st Alto Saxophone

LUDWIG VAN BEETHOVEN

Fantasie Impromptu

(Theme)

Mexican Hat Dance

The Glow Worm

1st Alto Saxophone

PAUL LINCKE